BE
CREATIVE

SCAN ME

OMFYI.COM

SCAN ME!

TO VIEW OUR BOOKS

SCAN ME!

TO VIEW OUR BOOKS

SCAN ME!

TO VIEW OUR BOOKS

PINK MOON COLORING BOOK - OM WOLF // OMFYI.COM

SCAN ME!:0

TO VIEW OUR BOOKS

SCAN ME!
TO VIEW OUR BOOKS

SCAN ME!
TO VIEW OUR BOOKS

SCAN ME!

TO VIEW OUR BOOKS

PINK MOON COLORING BOOK - OM WOLF // OMFYI.COM

SCAN ME!
TO VIEW OUR BOOKS

SCAN ME!

TO VIEW OUR BOOKS

SCAN ME!

TO VIEW OUR BOOKS

SCAN ME!

TO VIEW OUR BOOKS

PINK MOON COLORING BOOK - OM WOLF // OMFYI.COM

SCAN ME!

TO VIEW OUR BOOKS

SCAN ME!

TO VIEW OUR BOOKS

SCAN ME!

TO VIEW OUR BOOKS

SCAN ME!

TO VIEW OUR BOOKS

PINK MOON COLORING BOOK - OM WOLF // OMFYI.COM

Printed by Libri Plureos GmbH in Hamburg,
Germany